M000203732

B
B

God Can Handle It ...
For Kids

God Can Handle It ... For Kids

by Dr. S. M. Henriques

BRIGHTON BOOKS
Nashville, TN 37205
1-800-256-8584

ISBN 1-887655-91-3

The quoted ideas expressed in this book (but not scripture verses) are not, in all cases, exact quotations, as some have been edited for clarity and brevity. In all cases, the author has attempted to maintain the speaker's original intent. In some cases, quoted material for this book was obtained from secondary sources, primarily print media. While every effort was made to ensure the accuracy of these sources, the accuracy cannot be guaranteed. For additions, deletions, corrections or clarifications in future editions of this text, please write BRIGHTON BOOKS.

Printed in the United States of America

Layout by Sue Gerdes & Criswell Freeman
3 4 5 6 7 8 9 10 •   99 00 01

Scripture quotations marked (NIV)are taken from the HOLY BIBLE, NEW INTERNATIONAL VERSION ©. NIV ©. Copyright © 1973, 1978, 1984, by International Bible Society. Used by permission of Zondervan Publishing House. All rights reserved.

Scripture taken from *THE MESSAGE*. Copyright © 1993,1994,1995,1996. Used by permission of NavPress Publishing Group.

Scripture quoted from The Holy Bible, New Century Version, copyright 1987, 1988, 1991 by Word Publishing, Nashville, Tennessee. Used by permission

Scripture quoted from The Contempory English Version, copyright 1996, Thomas Nelson Publishers, Nashville, Tennessee. Used by permission.

For Jennifer and Jonathan

Table of Contents

Introduction

"Words of wisdom are like the stick a farmer uses to make animals move. These sayings come from God, our only shepherd, and they are like nails that fasten things together."
(Ecclesiastes 12:11, CEV)

Chapter 1

God Made You, and You Are Precious to Him.

You, and everyone else, were created in God's very own image.

So God created man in his own image, in the image of God he created him; male and female he created them.
Genesis 1:27 (NIV)

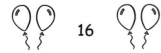 16

Every one of us is precious to God.

You are precious and honored
in my sight.
Isaiah 43:4a (NIV)

God knew who you were and what you were going to be, before you were even born.

With your own eyes you saw my body being formed. Even before I was born, you had written in your book everything I would do.
Psalm 139:16 (CEV)

18

Always remember that God made you just the way He wanted you to be. And God doesn't make any mistakes!

For he chose us in him before the creation
of the world to be holy and blameless
in his sight.
Ephesians 1:4a (NIV)

You are an original masterpiece of God. There is no one else exactly like you in all of creation.

I praise you because of the wonderful way you created me. Everything you do is marvelous! Of this I have no doubt.
Psalm 139:13 (CEV)

If a cow gives milk, it doesn't have to play the piano. You don't have to be or do everything, but do what you are good at doing.

And do not forget to do good and to share with others.
Hebrews 13:16a (NIV)

 21

Everything you do matters to God.

My dear friends, stand firm and don't be
shaken. Always keep busy working for the
Lord. You know that everything you do
for him is worthwhile.
1 Corinthians 15:58 (CEV)

God is constantly watching over you.

Nothing is hidden from God! He sees
through everything, and we will have
to tell him the truth.
Hebrews 4:13 (CEV)

God loves you so much He can't take His eyes off you!

The Lord is constantly watching everyone,
and he gives strength to those
who faithfully obey him.
2 Chronicles 16:9a (CEV)

Chapter 2

God Loves You
And Has a Great Plan
for You.

God created the world and the entire universe, and He has a perfect plan for it. God created you and has a wonderful plan for you, too ...

But what the LORD has planned will stand forever. His thoughts never change.
Psalm 33:11 (CEV)

 28

... an exciting plan!

"For I know the plans I have for you,"
declares the LORD, "plans to prosper you
and not to harm you, plans to give you
hope and a future."
Jeremiah 29:11 (NIV)

Since God cares so much for the insects and flowers, then we can know that He really does care for us, too!

God gives such beauty to everything that grows in the fields, even though it is here today and thrown into a fire tomorrow. He surely will do even more for you!
Matthew 6:30 (CEV)

30

At this very moment, God is working in your life to bring good to you.

And we know that all that happens to us is
working for our good if we love God
and are fitting into his plans.
Romans 8:28 (TLB)

You may stop loving God, but God never stops loving you...

I have loved you with an everlasting love.
Jeremiah 31:3a (NIV)

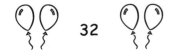

so remember this ....

God Can Handle It ... For Kids

God loves you!

So we know and rely on
the love God has for us.
God is love.
1 John 4:16a (NIV)

God loves us so much that He even calls us His children—because that is what we really are!

How great is the love the Father has lavished on us, that we should be called children of God! And that is what we are!
1 John 3:1a (NIV)

36

Nothing can come between you and God's love!

I am sure that nothing can separate us from God's love.
Romans 8:28a (CEV)

Every day, God's love
for you starts
all over again.
It never, never, never
gets old. Never!

Because of the LORD's great love we are not
consumed, for his compassions never fail.
They are new every morning;
great is your faithfulness.
Lamentations 3:22-23 (NIV)

38

There is no place you can go to escape God's love.

If I rise on the wings of the dawn, if I settle on the far side of the sea, even there your hand will guide me, your right hand will hold me fast.
Psalm 139:9-10 (NIV)

How high is the sky?

That's how much God loves you!

How great is God's love for all who worship
him? Greater than the distance
between heaven and earth!
Psalm 103:11 (CEV)

Chapter 3

God Never Makes A Mistake.

God always knows
exactly what
He is doing.

Exactly.

Always.

How many are your works, O LORD!
In wisdom you made them all;
the earth is full of your creatures.
Psalm 104:24 (NIV)

When you knock
on God's door,
He opens it
EVERY TIME...

... so don't be bashful about KNOCKING!

Everyone who asks, receives; all who seek,
find; and the door is opened
to everyone who knocks.
Luke 11:10 (TLB)

Sometimes God answers prayer by saying "no." Sometimes God answers prayer by saying "yes." Sometimes He answers prayer by saying "wait."

But one way or
the other, God always
answers prayer.

But God has surely listened and heard my
voice in prayer.
Psalm 66:19 (NIV)

 49

Sometimes we don't understand the things that happen to us, but ...

.... God will lead us if we trust Him.

I have shown you the way that makes sense;
I have guided you along the right path.
Proverbs 4:11 (CEV)

Are you confused or lost? God knows the way.

For this God is our God for ever and ever;
he will be our guide even to the end.
Psalm 48:14 (NIV)

52

Are you afraid about tomorrow? Jesus tells us not to worry.

Look at the birds in the sky! They don't plant or harvest. They don't even store grain in barns. Yet your Father in heaven takes care of them. Aren't you worth more than birds?
Matthew 6:26 (CEV)

Since God never
makes a mistake,
we can trust God for
everything we need.

This is the LORD, we trusted in him;
let us rejoice and be glad in his salvation.
Isaiah 25:9b (NIV)

Chapter 4

God Loves You
Even When You Make
Mistakes.

Everyone makes
mistakes.
Everyone!
So the next time you
make a mistake,
remember this ...

God Can Handle It ... For Kids

· ·

..............God loves you so much that not even your worst mistake can make Him change His mind about you.

The LORD does not look at the things man
looks at. Man looks at the outward
appearance, but the LORD
looks at the heart.
1 Samuel 16:7b (NIV)

 61

The next time you make a mistake, remember that God is very slow to get angry. Instead, He is full of kindness and love!

His love never fails.
Psalm 103:8b (CEV)

God loves us so much that He even sent His only Son, Jesus.

God loved the people of this world so much
that he gave his only Son, so that everyone
who has faith in him will have eternal life
and never really die.
John 3:16 (CEV)

 63

There is nothing you can do that will make God stop loving you.

I want you to know all about Christ's love,
although it is too wonderful to be measured.
Then your lives will be filled with
all that God is.
Ephesians 3:19 (CEV)

64

If we obey Him, God's Word can keep us from making many mistakes.

Your word is a lamp that gives light
wherever I walk.
Psalm 119:105 (CEV)

We make more mistakes when we are angry. So it is a good idea to control our tempers.

A wise man controls his temper.
He knows that anger causes mistakes.
Proverbs 14:29 (TLB)

To make mistakes is human; to keep on making the same old mistakes is not smart.

For all have sinned and fall short of the
glory of God.
Romans 3:23 (NIV)

Do the very best you can. Even angels cannot do better than that.

Therefore everyone who hears these words
of mine and puts them into practice is like a
wise man who built his house on the rock.
Matthew 7:24 (NIV)

Chapter 5

God Has Given Us Many Wonderful Gifts To Enjoy.

God created this beautiful world and everything in it.

God looked at what he had done.
All of it was very good!
Genesis 1:31a (CEV)

 72

All good things come from God.

Every good and perfect gift comes down
from the Father who created all the lights
in the heavens.
James 1:17 (CEV)

Each new day is ...

... a beautiful work of God.

This is the day the LORD has made; let us
rejoice and be glad in it.
Psalm 118:24 (NIV)

God's love for us is found in everything He does.

The LORD is good to all; he has compassion
on all he has made.
Psalm 145:9 (NIV)

 76

God really enjoys seeing His children laugh!

He will yet fill your mouth with laughter and
your lips with shouts of joy.
Job 8:21 (NIV)

 77

God blesses us so we can be a blessing to others.

I will bless you and make your name famous,
and you will be a blessing to many others.
Genesis 12:2b (TLB)

78

New life can be ours through Jesus Christ.

Because I live, you also will live.
John 14:19b (NIV)

What do you need? God invites you to talk to Him about it.

Ask and it will be given to you; seek and you will find; knock and the door will be opened to you.
Matthew 7:7 (NIV)

 81

If you ask Him, God will give you the wisdom you need to make the best choices for your life.

To the man who pleases him, God gives
wisdom, knowledge, and happiness.
Ecclesiastes 2:26a (NIV)

 82

Real peace comes only from God.

You will keep in perfect peace him whose
mind is steadfast, because he trusts in you.
Isaiah 26:3 (NIV)

 83

What we are is God's gift to us ....

84

...... what we make of ourselves is our gift to God.

Dear friends, God is good. So I beg you to offer your bodies to him as a living sacrifice, pure and pleasing. That's the most sensible way to serve God.
Romans 12:1 (CEV)

Chapter 6

God Is Always
Near Us.

No one can escape sadness. It happens to everyone sooner or later. But we can know that God is with us even during the sad times.

The Sovereign LORD will wipe away the tears from all faces.
Isaiah 25:8b (NIV)

88

Jesus never leaves us by ourselves — not even for one second.

I am with you always, even until
the end of the world.
Matthew 28:20 (CEV)

 89

When you want to be
near God with all your
heart, you can find
Him because ...

He's not playing hide-and-seek!

You will seek me and find me when you seek
me with all your heart.
Jeremiah 29:13 (NIV)

 91

Even when you are not aware of Him, God is there with you.

I will still be the same when you are old and
gray, and I will take care of you. I created
you. I will carry you and always
keep you safe.
Isaiah 46:4 (CEV)

92

God is one Friend who will never leave you.

The Lord has promised that he will not leave
us or desert us.
Hebrews 13:5b (CEV)

When bad things happen, remember that God is with you— even then!

Do not be afraid, for I am with you.
Isaiah 43:5a (NIV)

God is with us wherever we go.

I will be there to help you wherever you go.
Joshua 1:9b (CEV)

Chapter 7

We Can Trust God When We Are Afraid.

When you are afraid, remember that God loves you.

When I am afraid, I will trust in you.
Psalm 56:3 (NIV)

When everything else seems to be changing around you, remind yourself that Jesus never changes. You can count on Him to be the same every day of your life.

Jesus Christ is the same yesterday and today and forever.
Hebrews 13:8 (NIV)

Feeling afraid?

Remember that God is holding on to you tightly and will never let you go.

The eternal God is our hiding place; he
carries us in his arms.
Deuteronomy 33:27a (CEV)

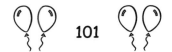 101

Trusting in God helps us to rise above the circumstances.

But those who hope in the LORD will renew their strength. They will soar on wings like eagles; they will run and not grow weary, they will walk and not faint.
Isaiah 40;31 (NIV)

102

Remember: no matter what the problem is, God wants to help.

God cares for you, so turn all your worries over to him.
1 Peter 5:7 (CEV)

Following God doesn't mean that we won't have problems.........

...................but.........

...following God <u>does</u> mean that when we have problems, He helps us.

In my distress I called to the LORD, and he answered me.
Jonah 2:2a (NIV)

 106

When you feel afraid, close your eyes and imagine yourself being held safely in God's great big hands.

He kept me safely hidden in
the palm of his hand.
Isaiah 49:2b (CEV)

108

When you are faced
with a big problem, it
is always a good idea
to be quiet in front of
God long enough for
Him to give you the
answer.

My soul finds rest in God alone; my salvation
· comes from him. He alone is my rock and my
salvation; he is my fortress,
I will never be shaken.
Psalm 62:1 (NIV)

Those who trust the Lord are given many, many blessings.

Blessed is the man who
makes the LORD his trust.
Psalm 40:4a (NIV)

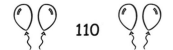

God sends His angels to watch over His children.

For he will command his angels concerning
you to guard you in all your ways.
Psalm 91:11 (NIV)

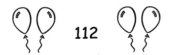

Trust God
for
everything.

Trust in the LORD forever, for the LORD
is the Rock eternal.
Isaiah 26:4 (NIV)

113

Chapter 8

Nothing Is
Too Hard
For God.

God always knows what you need.

Your Father knows what you need
before you ask him.
Matthew 6:8 (NIV)

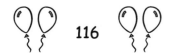

116

You can trust God in the little things and the big things.

You are my strong shield, and
I trust you completely.
Psalm 28:7a (CEV)

God never falls asleep on the job, nor is He too busy to listen to our prayers.

The LORD is your protector, and he won't go to sleep or let you stumble.
Psalm 121:3 (CEV)

God is so strong that He never gets tired of helping us.

Do you not know? Have you not heard? The LORD is the everlasting God, the Creator of the ends of the earth. He will not grow tired or weary, and his understanding no one can fathom.
Isaiah 40:28 (NIV)

 119

Nothing and no one is like God. When you need help, look to God instead of everywhere else.

There is none like the God of Jerusalem. He descends from the heavens in majestic splendor to help you.
Deuteronomy 33:26 (TLB)

120

God carries our
burdens when we ask
for His help.

God cares for you, so turn all your worries
over to him.
1 Peter 5:7 (CEV)

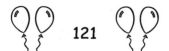

God always keeps His promises. He has never broken even one of them!

Deep in your hearts you know that the LORD
has kept every promise he ever made to you.
Not one of them has been broken.
Joshua 23:14b (CEV)

Chapter 9

God Tells Us How To Live For Him.

The Bible is an amazing Book that teaches us what we need to know about God.

Everything in the Scriptures is God's Word. All of it is useful for teaching and helping people and for correcting them and showing them how to live.
2 Timothy 3:16 (CEV)

God's Word shows us how to make right decisions.

Understanding your word brings light to the
minds of ordinary people.
Psalm 119:130 (CEV)

The Bible says that we can ask God to show us what He wants us to do.

If you want to know what God wants you to do, ask him, and he will gladly tell you, for he is always ready to give a bountiful supply of wisdom to all who ask him;
he will not resent it.
James 1:5 (TLB)

128

It is good to thank God and to praise Him.

Praise the LORD. How good it is to sing praises to our God, how pleasant and fitting to praise him!
Psalm 147:1 (NIV)

Put God first.............

...in everything you do.

Listen for God's voice in everything you do,
everywhere you go; he's the one who will
keep you on track.
Proverbs 3:6 (The Message)

Doing the right thing is better than having the right stuff.

A good reputation and respect are worth
much more than silver and gold.
Proverbs 22:1 (CEV)

 132

When other kids make fun of you, remember what Jesus told us to do about people like that.

Blessed are you when people insult you, persecute you and falsely say all kinds of evil against you because of me.
Matthew 5:11 (NIV)

133

Make the most of every opportunity to do good for someone else.

Therefore, as we have opportunity, let us do good to all people, especially to those who belong to the family of believers.
Galatians 6:10 (NIV)

 134

Keep praying, especially when times are tough.

Never stop praying.
1 Thessalonians 5:17 (CEV)

Jesus tells us to obey His words.

If anyone loves me, he will obey my teaching.
John 14:23a (NIV)

 136

If you're not sure about something, ask yourself: Tomorrow, will I be sorry I did this?

Be careful to do what is right in the eyes of everybody.
Romans 12:17b (NIV)

Who we really are shows up in the little things that we do and say.

Whatever you do, work at it with all your
heart, as working for the Lord, not for men.
Colossians 3:23 (NIV)

Whatever you do, give it your very best.

Whatever your hand finds to do, do it with
all your might.
Ecclesiastes 9:10a (NIV)

139

Chapter 9

God Tells Us How To Treat Others.

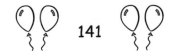

Treat others the way you want them to treat you.

Do to others as you would have them do to you.
Luke 6:31 (NIV)

 142

God Can Handle It ... For Kids

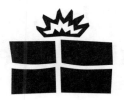

And here's an interesting question to ask yourself ...

God Can Handle It ... For Kids

. . . .

.....If God treated you tomorrow the way you treat others today, how would you feel?

Each of us should please his neighbor for his good, to build him up.
Romans 15:2 (NIV)

The way we treat others shows what kind of people we really are.

The good or bad that children do
shows what they are like.
Proverbs 20:11 (CEV)

147

We show our love for others in the way we treat them.

Love one another deeply, from the heart.
1 Peter 1:22b (NIV)

148

God blesses us when we are kind to those who say unkind things about us.

Do not repay evil with evil or insult with insult, but with blessing, because to this you were called so that you may inherit a blessing.
1 Peter 3:9 (NIV)

149

Be patient with the faults of others; they have to be patient with yours.

We who are strong ought to bear with the
failings of the weak and not
to please ourselves.
Romans 15:1 (NIV)

Ask God to help you be kind to everyone ... even little brothers and sisters.

Be kind and compassionate to one another,
forgiving each other, just as in Christ
God forgave you.
Ephesians 4:32 (NIV)

 151

We should be honest with everyone.

The Lord hates cheating and delights
in honesty.
Proverbs 11:1 (TLB)

 152

Never grow tired of doing what is right.

Don't get tired of helping others. You will be
rewarded when the time is right,
if you don't give up.
Galatians 6:9 (CEV)

Remember:

God expects us to show our love for others by our actions.

Dear children, let us not love with words or
tongue but with actions and in truth.
1 John 3:18 (NIV)

 155

In Conclusion

"Everything you were taught can be put into a few words: Respect and obey God! This is what life is all about."
Ecclesiastes 12:13 (CEV)

The End

About the Author

Dr. S. M. Henriques, known to his friends as "Rocky," lives and writes in Jackson, Mississippi. He is a graduate of New Orleans Baptist Theological Seminary with 20 years experience as a pastor.

Dr. Henriques is the author of *God Can Handle It ... Marriage* and *God Can Handle It For Kids,* both published by Brighton Books. He is also publisher of *The Timothy Report,* an internet newsletter for pastors. Dr. Henriques is married with two children.

About the God Can Handle It Series

This book is part of a series called God Can Handle It. Each book in this collection combines inspirational quotations with relevant scripture passages. For more information about these or other titles from Brighton Books, please call 800-256-8584.